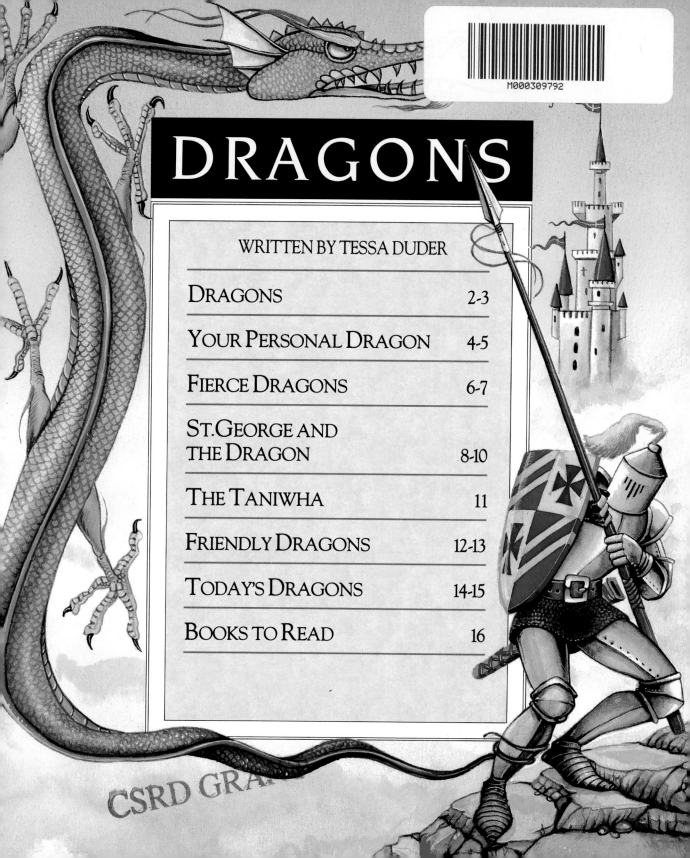

DRAGONS

WRITTEN BY TESSA DUDER

CSRD GRA

DRAG

When you picture

Is he kind or is he scary,
Is he smooth or very hairy?

◆

Is he old and fierce and wary,
Or is he young, contemporary?

Does he want to help a friend

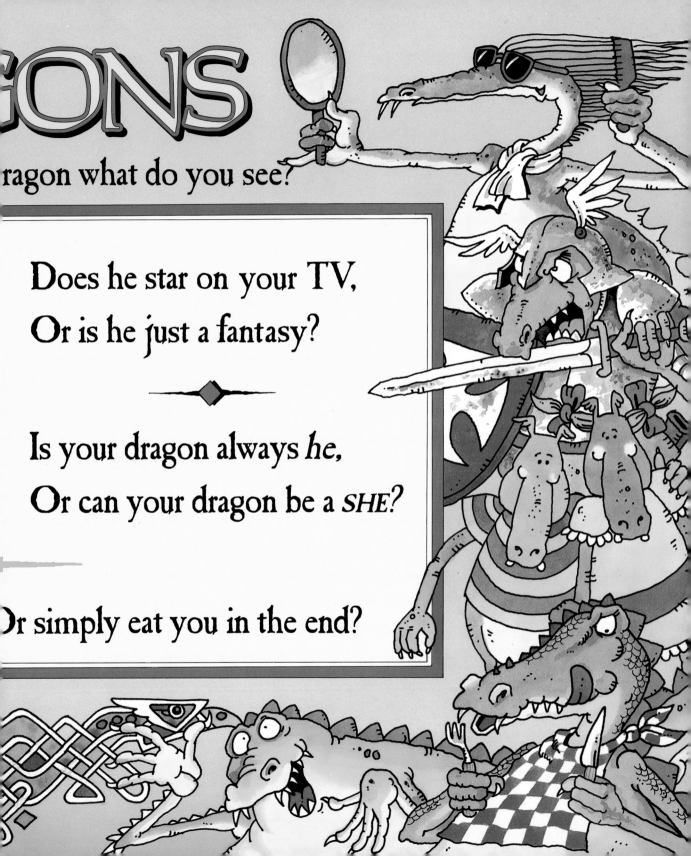

ᏀONS

ragon what do you see?

Does he star on your TV,
Or is he just a fantasy?

◆

Is your dragon always *he*,
Or can your dragon be a *SHE?*

Or simply eat you in the end?

People have always talked of dragons. They always will, as long as people dream dreams and tell their stories to each other.

Dragon is an interesting word. It came to English from an old Greek word, *drakon*, meaning snake. Over two thousand years later, the word *dragon* is often used to describe many sorts of monsters.

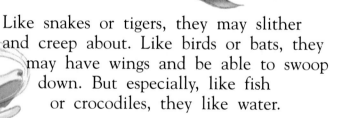

Like snakes or tigers, they may slither and creep about. Like birds or bats, they may have wings and be able to swoop down. But especially, like fish or crocodiles, they like water.

No one really knows why so many people believe in dragons.

Some think that dragon stories help to explain how the world began, or why there are mists and thunder and storms.

4

Perhaps dragons are needed to explain the fear people have of particularly dangerous or unpleasant animals— snakes, crocodiles, tigers, large birds, toads, and bats. Put pieces of them together and you've got a dragon.

Perhaps there is a connection with the worship of snakes, found in most countries in the world. Snakes are connected with immortality, death, wisdom and healing.

Or perhaps dragons are a distant memory of the giant reptiles which millions of years ago used to rule the world.

Everyone's idea of a dragon is different. Many countries have stories about their own special dragons.

5

FIERCE

We tend to think of dragons as male, but the first dragon was Tiamat, a fierce female dragon with a snake-like body, legs, and horns. She appeared over three thousand years ago in a famous creation story from Babylonia.

After some terrible family quarrels, Tiamat's son Marduk killed her by shooting an arrow through her heart. Marduk, who became ruler of the universe, used half of Tiamat's body to make the sky and the other half to make the earth.

Since Tiamat, there have been many other stories of conflict between a dragon, representing evil and chaos, and a hero, representing good and order. These evil dragons came in all shapes and sizes, but they were usually heavy and ugly, creatures of darkness.

DRAGONS

The seven-headed Hydra was one of the dragons of ancient Greece. The Greeks had other dragons, Ladon and Typhon, as well as a whole bunch of dragons called Titans.

In Scandinavia there was the "Dread Biter," Midhoggr, who spent his time gnawing at the tree of the universe, trying to kill it. In Germany there was Fafnir, a giant who turned into a dragon to guard his gold and who was finally killed by the hero Siegfried. In Islamic countries there was the fierce dragon Thu'ban with flaming eyes and many teeth.

St. George
AND THE
Dragon

 NE of the most famous dragons didn't have a name. He was simply "The Dragon slain by St. George."

The usual story tells of a deadly dragon who lived in a lake and had such bad breath that he poisoned all the countryside around. To keep him quiet, the people had to feed him two sheep every day. When all the sheep were gone, it was the children's turn, and finally the turn of the king's daughter. Like those before her, she was left in a field near the lake, bound to a stake, waiting to be eaten.

Enter our hero, a passing soldier named George. The princess told him what was about to happen to her. "Run for your life," she said. "There is no point in both of us being eaten."

But George waited. The dragon came for his dinner. There was a short battle. The dragon was wounded so badly that George was able to bind him with the princess' silken sash and take him back to the city for the people to see. Finally George lopped his head off.

Historians think that George was a real soldier who lived in the second century A.D. Later he was made the patron saint of England. Slaying the dragon was just one of his heroic acts. April 23, the day his own head was cut off by the Emperor of Persia, is still remembered as St. George's Day.

10

THE TANIWHA

The Maori people of New Zealand have many legends about their dragons, the taniwha*. One story tells of the warrior Tamure and the taniwha, Kaiware, who lived in a blowhole cave at Piha.

Kaiware was a fierce taniwha who often killed and ate people who came to fish nearby. Tamure said, "With my magic greenstone mere†, I will kill this taniwha!"

He hid near the taniwha's cave and waited while some of his tribe went by the cave, pretending to fish. When Kaiware came out of his cave to catch the men, Tamure struck him with his mere, wounding the taniwha so badly that he fled away and never returned.

You can still see the blowhole and the wide rock which the wounded Kaiware flattened with his mighty tail as he fought with Tamure.

*pronounced tan'ee-fah   †a short fighting club

FRIENDLY

Eastern dragons are quite different from fierce Western dragons. They are usually kind, elegant—even helpful—creatures of water and mists. Their brightly colored skins glow at night.

CHINESE DRAGONS

The Chinese dragon has been very carefully described. It has four legs, a long snake-like body, but usually no wings. It is made up of nine different animals.

It is deaf, fond of eating sparrows and swallows, and is afraid of centipedes and things made of iron. Under its chin is a pearl. Its breath changes into clouds from which come either fire or rain. Sometimes it takes human form. It is thunder and lightning and mists.

DRAGONS

INDIAN DRAGONS

Indian dragons, called nagas, are also water-gods but especially connected with rain and rivers.

Like Chinese dragons, they wear a pearl, but on their foreheads. They live in fine palaces below the sea or at the bottom of lakes. They are not always friendly. When annoyed, they can kill people with their breath or cause droughts.

There is an Indian dragon-slaying myth too. The dragon Vritra holds the rains in his belly. It takes Indra, the weather-god, to shoot a thunderbolt at Vritra and release the rain.

TODAY'S

L et's think about today's dragons.

Chinese children enjoy the long dragon made of bamboo and cloth appearing at Chinese New Year. At Nanking in southern China the Dragon Boat Regatta has been held on the fifth day of the fifth moon for over 2000 years.

Japanese and Malaysian children enjoy flying dragon kites.

Indonesian children know their country has about the nearest thing to a living dragon. It is the komodo dragon, a large forked-tongued lizard which lives on a small group of islands.

It grows up to four meters long, swims, and lays eggs. Its food is birds and small animals, but it can also be dangerous to people.

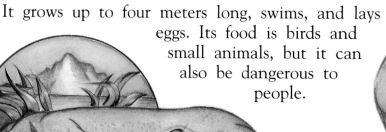

DRAGONS

Scottish children have their famous Loch Ness Monster, a lake-dragon first seen in the sixth century. So far no one has managed to catch it.

In the meantime, we can catch familiar dragons and new dragons in our minds. There are many stories about dragons in books. Some are scary, but many are lovable clumsy creatures too, not quite coping with today's world. Modern writers like J. R. Tolkien, Margaret Mahy, and Michael Ende have dreamed up new dragons. There are also lots of well-known board games featuring dragons.

And ever since the invention of movies, film makers have created all sorts of amazing dragons. What films with dragons have you seen? You probably know more dragons than you think.

Did you know. . . Dragon medicines did wonderful things in ancient China. They were made of dragon bones, teeth, brain, liver, and blood. "Dragon spit" was used to make perfume. "Dragon fat" burned as very bright lamps.

BOOKS TO READ

I f you want to read more about dragons and see many colorful pictures of them, here are some suggestions:

The Book of the Dragon
  Time-Life Books,
  Chartwell Books, 1979

The Flight of Dragons
  Peter Dickinson,
  Harper & Row, 1979

Dragons
  Peter J. Hogarth,
  Viking Press, 1979

The Dragon and the Disk;
An Investigation into the
Totally Fantastic
  F.W. Holiday,
  Norton, 1973

Dragons and Unicorns:
A Natural History
  Paul A. Johnsgaard,
  St. Martin's Press, 1982

A Lion in the Meadow
  Margaret Mahy,
  Overlook Press, Woodstock, NY, 1992

A Book of Dragons
  Ruth Manning-Sanders,
  Dutton, 1965

Fabulous Beasts and Demons
  Heinz Mode,
  Phaidon (London), Praeger
  (New York), 1975

The Hill of the Dragon: An Inquiry into
the Nature of Dragon Legends
  Paul Newman,
  Rowman and Littlefield, 1979

Dragons, Unicorns, and Other
Magical Beasts
  Robin Palmer,
  Henry Z. Walck Inc., 1966

The Evolution of the Dragon
  G. Elliot Smith,
  Albert Saifer, 1918

Dragons
  The Enchanted World
  Time-Life Books, 1984